MW01230921

CHUTZPAH HEROES

CHUTZPAH HEROES

THIRTEEN STORIES ABOUT UNDERDOGS WITH WIT AND COURAGE

WILLIAM J EDGAR

XULON ELITE

Xulon Press Elite
555 Winderley Pl, Suite 225
Maitland, FL 32751
407.339.4217
www.xulonpress.com

© 2024 by William J Edgar

All rights reserved solely by the author. The author guarantees all contents are original and do not infringe upon the legal rights of any other person or work. No part of this book may be reproduced in any form without the permission of the author.

Due to the changing nature of the Internet, if there are any web addresses, links, or URLs included in this manuscript, these may have been altered and may no longer be accessible. The views and opinions shared in this book belong solely to the author and do not necessarily reflect those of the publisher. The publisher therefore disclaims responsibility for the views or opinions expressed within the work.

Unless otherwise indicated, Scripture quotations taken from the Good News Bible © 1994 published by the Bible Societies/HarperCollins Publishers Ltd UK, Good News Bible© American Bible Society 1966, 1971, 1976, 1992. Used with permission.

Paperback ISBN-13: 978-1-66289-714-6
Ebook ISBN-13: 978-1-66289-715-3

Dedication

This collection of thirteen stories is dedicated to five grandchildren, Julian, Owen, Nathaniel, Eleanor, and Luke. At ages eight, six, four, six, and three, they listened raptly to two of these stories as I told them one summer outside our small cabin in the Catskill Mountains of New York. Their attentiveness sparked the idea for this book.

Table of Contents

Acknowledgements

I am indebted to Susan Edgar, mother of Julian, Owen, and Nathaniel, for her invaluable help in writing these stories. She steered me back towards oral story telling style when I would veer towards standard written English. She added her own touches. Of course, I am also indebted to The Living God who inspired the first writers of these true stories, Moses, the prophets, and the Gospel writers.

Exact Bible quotations are taken from *Good News Bible*, American Bible Society, and are duly referenced. Where the Hebrew has YHWH, the author follows the convention of most English translations and renders it as LORD. Most sentences in quotation marks, however, are the author's story-telling version of the Bible's stories. The alert reader will occasionally notice echoes of the King James Version. At the beginning of each chapter the main Bible source of its contents is given.

Introduction

Fathers and mothers, these stories are for your children. They will teach them confidence in God, so that they can think how to act in new, and maybe desperate, situations. Those who trust in the Lord need not live in fear. God has promised, "I will never leave you; I will never abandon you (Hebrews 13:5)." Fifteen-year-old David sees Goliath and knows, "With God's help, I can take him!" Eight-year-old Miriam sees Pharaoh's daughter look pityingly at her baby brother in his tiny boat and runs without hesitation through the bulrushes to ask the Princess, "Would you like me to find a nurse for him among the Hebrew women?" The blind, the old, children, and social outcasts appear in this book.

Here are three ways to use this book, but don't let the best way be the enemy of the good.

Good Way
Give this book to your child to read.
Better Way
Read this book to your child. Reading to your child before bedtime is one of the delights of life, both for you and for your child.
Best Way
Read the story, maybe to yourself or maybe to your child. Then later tell the story to your child as it comes out of your mind and mouth. Create the scenes with your words, tones, and gestures. Your child will soon have a favorite story and will ask you to tell it again, and again,

and again. My seven-year-old granddaughter Eleanor has three younger brothers and three boy cousins whom she sees constantly. Her favorite story is about a woman called "blessed above all women" – not Mary the Mother of Jesus, but Jael who killed Sisera with a tent peg through his temple. She can't hear this story often enough.

Why call them "Chutzpah Heroes?" "Chutzpah" (hard H initial sound) is a Yiddish word describing an arrogant person full of insolent nerve. But in English conversation, chutzpah describes the ability to size up a situation quickly, see what can be done, and have the guts to do it. Practical wisdom + bravery – that is chutzpah!

In the coming days your children will need wisdom and bravery. Our society collapses under the burden of untamed young men, ubiquitous drugs, ubiquitous pornography, and gambling available on every smart phone. Getting married and having children terrifies many. Disconnected and discontented people are determined to tear their world apart and start over again. Our rulers have lost their way. Underneath it all, there is no fear of God and thus little hope for the future. Our children will need the chutzpah to stand bravely and wisely, encouraged by knowing that they are not alone. The unseen God and his mighty angels, often along with families and churches, stand with them.

Here is a family story. A history teacher in our local public high school was talking about Bible classes he was required to take at two very different colleges. At the second, more enlightened school, when they read about lifespans of hundreds of years in Genesis 5, the teacher explained that the writer of Genesis meant lunar months, not solar years. My oldest son saw opportunity. He raised his hand. "It also says that they began having children when they were eighty. That sounds pretty old for starting to have kids, but if you divide eighty by thirteen you get...." The whole class laughed while the teacher slowly divided thirteen into eighty on the blackboard to find first child born when father was six years old. Nine years later, son's younger brother had the same teacher. After three days, his classmates asked him, "Why does the teacher hate you so much?"

He endured this tiny bit of suffering, the legacy of his older brother's chutzpah. Both boys knew that their family and church stood with them.

The stories in this book will teach your children how to run with men so that when the time requires it they can run with horses (see Jeremiah 12:5). Their heroes embody the wit to see quickly what to do and courage to do it. Underlying godly chutzpah is faith in the living God.

David the Shepherd

"I Can Take Him"

I Samuel 17

D avid was about fifteen when the Philistines invaded Israel with a new super-weapon, a giant named Goliath. David's three oldest brothers joined King Saul to fight the Philistines in the Valley of Elah. David stayed home in Bethlehem to watch his family's sheep in the wilderness out beyond the village's fields.

What did a shepherd do? First, he led his sheep to grass and water. Second, he protected them from wild animals and thieves. Third, he herded his sheep at night into a pen made of big stones with no roof, and he slept on the ground at the only entrance to keep wild animals out and the sheep in. In those days shepherds had no sheep dogs to help them, and there were no fences. Shepherds carried one weapon, a stick with a leather sling attached to its end. With this weapon, David could do two things. With the stick he could beat animals that came too close to his sheep and with the sling he could throw stones at those threatening to come near. All in all, being a shepherd was a boring job, except when a lion or a bear tried to grab a sheep or a lamb, or when a sheep wandered off and David had to retrieve it.

After the war was about six weeks old, David's father, Jesse, called him. "Take roasted grain and ten loaves of bread to your brothers. And take these ten cheeses to their commander. See how your brothers are doing." David put the food on a donkey and left with the first light of morning, walking up and down hills to the Valley of Elah.

When David got to the Israelite camp, both armies were lining up on opposite sides of the valley. Near the valley's bottom ran a stream. David left the food with the man who kept the supplies and ran to look for his brothers. Then Goliath strode out from the Philistine line. He shouted. "I am a Philistine. You are slaves of Saul. Send me a man and we will fight. If your man wins, we will be your slaves. If I win, you will be our slaves. I dare you to send a man to fight me!" Who would dare to fight Goliath? He wore bronze armor weighing over 200 pounds and had a bronze helmet. Bronze is made from copper and tin mixed together and it is very hard. Goliath also had a spear as big as a cloth weaver's beam, a javelin, and of course a sword. A man went in front of him to carry his shield.

While Goliath strutted and shouted, David listened to the scared soldiers around him. "Do you see him? He's humongous. King Saul says he will reward whoever kills him, let him marry his daughter, and his family will never pay taxes again." David talked to one man after another. "Really?" he asked, "Tell me again what reward goes to the man who kills that uncircumcised Philistine." Eliab, David's oldest brother, sneered at him. "What are you doing asking all these questions? You just came to watch the battle. Why aren't you with those few sheep of yours in the wilderness?" "Can't I even ask a few questions?" David said and went right on talking. Remember, David was fifteen. That's how fifteen-year-old boys answer their big brothers.

Someone told King Saul about David. "Bring him to me," Saul ordered. "Are you ready to fight this Philistine?" he asked. David answered politely. "Your Majesty, no one should be afraid. Your servant will fight this Philistine." Saul could see this boy had chutzpah, but what could he do against the giant warrior Goliath? But David saw something the regular soldiers did not see. With a shepherd's sling, he could attack Goliath from a distance until he put a stone right between his eyes. Unencumbered by armor, David could run and keep away from Goliath's weapons as they fought their single combat. Most importantly, David knew that the God of Israel was with him. Goliath did not stand a chance, but only David saw that. He would do what everyone else thought was crazy. He would fight Goliath.

Saul said, "You're just a boy!" David answered, "Your servant once killed a bear trying to take one of my lambs. Another time I killed a lion when it turned on me. I grabbed it and beat it to death. And I can kill this Philistine who defies the armies of the Living God. The Lord who saved me from the paw of the bear and the paw of the lion will save me from this uncircumcised Philistine."

So Saul agreed to let David fight. He offered David his armor. David politely tried it on, walked a few steps, and said, "I am not used to it." David took it off. Soon both armies saw a shepherd boy picking his way down the rocky hill. He was armed only with a stick and a sling at its end. At the stream, David stopped and chose five smooth stones. He put them into his shepherd's bag.

David walked down the valley by himself, but he wasn't alone. Behind him was a whole army that could not imagine him winning, but desperately wanted him to. His older brothers were watching, maybe remembering that they had seen the prophet Samuel pour olive oil on David's head to anoint him as Israel's next king. David was fighting for his family. He was fighting for his home, Bethlehem. He was fighting for the whole People of God, and God was with him. David did not know that God's unseen angels were also with him, but they were. David walked alone, but no, he was not alone.

When Goliath saw David, he sneered. "Am I a dog, that you come to fight me with sticks? Come here, boy, and I will feed your body to the vultures and the wild animals." And Goliath cursed David in the name of his gods. David boasted back better than Goliath. "You have a sword and a spear, but I come in the name of the LORD, whose armies you insult. He will give me victory. I will cut off your head, and give the corpses **of**

your whole army to the birds and animals for food. Then everyone will know that there is a God in Israel." By now the two armies were hardly breathing, watching the soldier and the boy.

David ran towards Goliath, chose a stone from his bag, put it in his sling at the end of his stick, and slung it at Goliath with all his might. It went right to the spot on Goliath's head that his helmet did not cover, his forehead between his eyes right at the top of his nose. Goliath tumbled forward. For a moment, there was no sound except thousands of men sucking in their breath in astonishment. David ran right to Goliath, pulled out Goliath's own sword, raised it above his head, and brought it down with all his might. He cut off Goliath's head! In a last act of chutzpah, David knocked off Goliath's helmet, and picked up his head by its hair. He held it high above his head for all to see. Goliath was dead!

The soldiers of Israel shouted a tremendous war cry that echoed up and down the valley and raced down the hill to attack. The Philistines turned and ran. After killing a lot of Philistines and chasing them back to their cities, the Israelites took the food, clothing, and weapons their enemies had left behind.

An amazed and happy King Saul said to his General, named Abner, "Whose son is that boy? Bring him to me." So Abner brought David, still holding Goliath's bloody head. "Whose son are you, young man?" Saul asked. David answered, "I am the son of your servant Jesse, in Bethlehem." The King said, "Don't go home. From now on, stay with me." Soon that brave fifteen-year-old boy was Saul's best army commander. Fifteen years later when King Saul died, David, the shepherd boy, became Israel's second and greatest king.

Miriam the Big Sister

"Shall I Call a Hebrew Nurse?"

Exodus 2:1-10

The day Miriam had been dreading began like every day in Egypt. A hot sun lit the dry eastern sky. Eight-year-old Miriam had a beautiful baby brother whom she loved to snuggle and kiss. Today she would lose him. The baby's mother, Jochabed, had finished a small boat for her son. She wove it from the reeds that grow near the Nile River and covered it with tar. It had a small lid. Today mother would put her son into the boat and put the boat into the water by the bank of the Nile River.

Why would Miriam's mother do that? Miriam knew. It was because he was a boy! Egypt's king, called Pharaoh, was afraid Hebrew boys would grow up to fight against him some day. So he told the Hebrew midwives to kill every Hebrew baby boy, but let the girls live. The brave midwives disobeyed Pharaoh and let the boys live. They lied to Pharaoh. "The Hebrew women are not like Egyptian women. They give birth very fast, before we get to them, so we can't kill the boys." So Pharaoh tried something different. He told the Egyptians, "Any baby Hebrew boy you see or hear, throw him into the River."

What could a Hebrew family do when it had a boy? Miriam's family hid their baby son for as long as they dared, but after three months he cried too loudly not to be heard. Soon the Egyptian neighbors would hear him and come to throw him into the River. So Miriam's mother made a boat for the baby to float away on the Nile River. He would be in the River as Pharaoh commanded, but in a boat and in God's hands.

As the sun came up, Miriam and her mother carried boat and baby through the reeds to the river's edge. Miriam kissed her baby brother one last time. Jochabed laid her baby in the boat and put the boat into the water. Miriam's mother said to her, "Stay here and see what happens. I'm going home. I can't watch." Miriam hid among the reeds beside the river. Alone, she watched. Would the boat float out to sea? Would it spring a leak and sink? Who knew? Only God did! Miriam never could have imagined what happened next.

In the distance came voices and laughter. Pharaoh's daughter was coming with her servants to take a bath in the Nile River. The Princess saw the tiny boat floating among the reeds and was curious. "Bring me that little boat," she ordered one of her servants. The servant waded through the water and got the boat. When the Princess lifted the boat's lid, she saw a gorgeous baby boy. He began to cry, and the Princess's heart melted.

In a flash, Miriam knew what to do and bravely did it. She ran straight through the reeds to the Princess. Hebrew slaves, however young, knew not to approach the Princess, certainly not without being called. Doing that could cost them their lives. Even ordinary Egyptians knew not to run right up to Pharaoh's daughter and start talking to her. But Miriam did just that.

"Would you like me to get a woman from the Hebrews to nurse the baby for you?" she asked. Likely laughing because she knew who the nurse would be, the Princess said, "Yes, do that. I will pay her to nurse this baby for me." So off Miriam ran as fast as she could to get her mother. "Mother," she said breathlessly. "Come right now! Pharaoh's daughter wants you to nurse our baby." So Jochabed ran to the River Nile with Miriam. The Princess ordered her, "Take this baby and nurse him for me. I will pay you." So the baby boy rescued by Pharaoh's daughter went home with his own mother. Pharaoh's daughter would protect her son from being put into the river again.

In those days mothers nursed their children for years, not months. As the boy grew, Jochabed told him stories. She told him he was a Hebrew who served the God of Abraham, Isaac, and Jacob. He also learned that he belonged to the Princess, Pharaoh's daughter. She had saved him. Finally, the boy stopped nursing – which is called weaning -- and the Princess sent for him. His mother may well have gone along to continue caring for him. The Princess named him Moses, because she had fished him out of the water.

Moses lived with the Princess at the palace until he was forty years old, and he learned all the wisdom of the Egyptians. But one day Moses decided to side with Hebrew slaves against their cruel Egyptian masters. He killed an Egyptian boss who was mistreating the slaves. Fearing for his life, Moses ran away to the Sinai desert, got married, became a shepherd, and had two sons. He was contented.

But! When Moses was eighty years old, God told him to go back to Egypt with a message for Pharaoh, "Let my people go." Pharaoh said, "Not a chance. I don't know this God of yours." But after God sent ten plagues on Egypt, Pharaoh said, "Go." Miriam went too. Pharaoh quickly changed his mind and ordered his army to bring his slaves back. The army chased after Israel and trapped them against the Red Sea, but God opened the waters and Israel crossed over on dry land. Pharaoh's soldiers followed, but God sent the waters back and drowned Pharaoh's army just like baby Moses was supposed to be drowned.

When they knew they were finally safe, eighty-eight-year-old Miriam joyously grabbed her tambourine. She led Israel, singing, "Sing to the LORD, for he has triumphed gloriously. The horse and his rider has he thrown into the sea." Old Miriam surely remembered how long ago she had bravely rushed through the reeds to speak to Pharaoh's daughter. She was only eight years old when she did that!

Bartimaeus, a Blind Man

"I Want to See"

Mark 10:46-52, Matthew 20:19-24

B artimaeus was blind. He lived in Jericho, an ancient city on the western plains of the Jordan River. Jericho is the lowest city in the world, 850 feet below sea level and a little north from the Dead Sea. Jericho was also on the desolate and winding mountain road pilgrims climbed to get to the Temple in Jerusalem.

Bartimaeus sat next the road with a blind friend. These two blind men loved Passover time in the spring. Lots of people came by them then. It was the best time for begging. Passover for the beggars of Jericho was like Christmas for American stores. It's when they made the most money.

Blind people hear everything because they see nothing. They rely on touch, smell, and hearing. Is a crowd coming? Is someone riding a donkey? Is a person alone or with a family? Are rich, important people coming? Blind beggars know the answers to these questions from the sounds coming down the road. Blind beggars also know far more news than one might think. They hear people talking even when they think no one is listening, and they remember what they hear.

One spring day Bartimaeus and his friend heard a very large and excited crowd coming. Their accents showed they were Galileans, like most of the pilgrims that came on this road to Jerusalem. Soon Bartimaeus knew Jesus was in the crowd. He had passed through Jericho before. Bartimaeus knew about Jesus' miracles and teaching. Common people loved to tell stories about his miracles and about how he had bested educated Pharisees in argument. He knew hope was building that Jesus was the promised Messiah, the coming Son of David who would save Israel. Of course, by Jesus' day there were thousands of men who were descended from David. But Jesus had the healing hands of a king. And he preached, "The Kingdom of God is near. Repent and believe this wonderful announcement." Maybe Bartimaeus had heard some of Jesus' preaching from his Sermon on the Mount, such as, "Ask, you will receive; seek, and you will find; knock, and the door will be opened to you (Matthew 7:7)."

The crowd came close to the blind beggars. Some probably dropped a few coins into their cups and Bartimaeus mumbled his thanks. "May the God of Israel bless you." But when Jesus got near, Bartimaeus saw his chance. He knew Jesus could heal him. He would ask, seek, and knock as loudly as he could.

Bartimaeus began screaming, "Jesus! Son of David! Take pity on me!" People nearby scolded him. They said, "Shush. You are making a nuisance of yourself. Be quiet." But Bartimaeus' non-stop shouting meant, "I know who you are. I know you can hear me. I know you can help me if you want to." The more people told Bartimaeus to be quiet, the louder he shouted. He had chutzpah. He wasn't going to lose his chance to see again. "Jesus! Son of David! Have pity on me!" "Jesus! Son of David! Have pity on me!" "Jesus! Son of David! Have pity on me!" He was very annoying. Maybe he even embarrassed his blind friend who begged with him every day.

Suddenly Jesus stopped and the crowd stopped with him. Jesus said to a few disciples, "Call him." The crowd was now suddenly on Bartimaeus' side. Jesus had called for him. They said, "Cheer up. He has called for you." Bartimaeus and his blind friend threw off their cloaks and jumped up. With help from their new friends in the crowd, they came to Jesus. Jesus asked Bartimaeus one question. "What do you want me to do for you?" Of course, he knew what Bartimaeus wanted, but God wants us to tell him our needs and ask for help. God wants us to pray to him.

Bartimaeus said to Jesus, "Teacher, I want to see again." "Go," Jesus said. "Go, your faith has made you well." Immediately Bartimaeus could see again, the way he had as a boy. Jesus healed Bartimaeus' friend too.

Bartimaeus joined the crowd on the climb to Jerusalem, seeing and walking and talking and talking and talking. Instead of his former drone, "Alms for the poor, alms for the poor," he had an exciting story to tell. It was about how Jesus, the Son of David, had restored his sight and now he could **SEE**.

About ten weeks later, Bartimaeus probably became part of the new church. He told how Jesus gave him his sight again and again. The Gospel writers wrote it down. Bartimaeus' story became part of the Good News about Jesus the Son of David. In fact, Christians were soon telling Bartimaeus' story all over the Roman Empire! They tell it today all over the world.

King Saul the Farmer

"Tomorrow You Will Be Saved"

I Samuel 8 - 11

O ur country doesn't have a king, not since George III of England long ago. We got rid of him and became a republic. But kings have ruled most countries through most of history. How does a man become a king? The easiest way is to be the son of a king. The hardest way is to be the first king in a country that never had one. King Saul of Israel was Israel's first king, and it took a lot for him to become king. God chose him. But the people only really accepted him as king when he suddenly acted with kingly chutzpah and won a war. Here is how Saul became king.

Until Saul, God ruled Israel with judges. The last judge was a great prophet named Samuel. But when he got old, the people came to him and said, "You are old and your sons are not like you. We want a king like other nations have, to fight our battles for us." Samuel didn't like what the people said, but God told him to do it. How?

First, some donkeys belonging to Saul's father Kish wandered off. Saul went to find them. When Saul was about to give up looking, his servant said, "Let's ask the man of God who lives near here about the donkeys. Everything he says comes true." So they got directions to the man of God's house. In the meantime, God told Samuel that he would soon send him

Israel's new king. When Samuel saw Saul, the LORD said to him, "This is the one." Immediately Samuel said to Saul, "Your donkeys have been found. But whom does Israel want? Is it not you and your family?" Saul said humbly, "I'm from the smallest tribe, Benjamin. How can this be?" The next day Samuel took out a jar of olive oil and anointed Saul as king by pouring the oil on Saul's head. But Saul was certainly not king yet in the people's eyes. They did not even know what Samuel had done.

Next, Samuel called Israel to meet at a place called Mizpah. He scolded Israel for asking for a king, but then said God would give them one. Samuel "cast lots" – sort of like rolling dice -- and the lot chose the tribe of Benjamin. The second lot chose one of Benjamin's clans, the third lot chose the family of Kish, and the final lot chose Saul. Saul could see that he would be chosen and he did not want to be king. So he hid among the baggage, but he was soon discovered and brought to Samuel. Samuel shouted, "Here is the man the LORD has chosen. There is no one else like him." People shouted, "Long live the king!" Then Samuel explained the rights and duties of a king and sent everyone home.

However, even though Saul was tall and handsome, he was a farmer and did not know how to be a king. He had no army. He had no government. So the new king of Israel went back to farming. Some king! Still, a few men whom God touched stayed with him.

Then something terrible happened on the east side of the Jordan River, in Gilead. King Nahash of Ammon attacked the Israelites who lived there and chased them into their walled city, Jabesh-Gilead. Defeated, the men of Gilead offered to make a treaty with the Ammonites and be their servants. But that wasn't good enough for Nahash. "Okay, but you must first let us put out the right eye of every man in your city." With their right eyes gouged or burned out, most of the men would not be good at fighting. Their blind right eye would also humiliate them. For the rest of their lives, those blind right eyes would shout, "Loser," to their wives, their children, and of course the Ammonites.

The men of Jabesh-Gilead did not want to lose their right eyes, but what could they do? "Alright, we agree," they answered, "but give us time to see if our brothers across the Jordan River will come help us." Nahash said okay because when Israel to the west of the Jordan River did not help, he would look even greater. So, with only a sliver of hope, Jabesh-Gilead sent a messenger to that new king, Saul of Gibeah -- but what could he do? He was a farmer!

The messengers told their story to the people of Gibeah where Saul lived. Everybody started crying and wailing, but no one knew what to do. Just then Saul returned from the fields, walking behind his oxen. "What is wrong?" he asked. They told him.

When Saul heard the story, the spirit of God came on him and filled him with anger. He suddenly knew what to do and did it. He took his two oxen, which belonged to his father, and cut them in pieces. They cost a lot of money and without them a farmer was poor. It was like cutting your tractor into pieces!

The people watched Saul kill the oxen and cut them up. It was hard and bloody work. What was Saul up to? What would his father Kish say? Then Saul sent one bloody ox piece to every tribe of Israel with this message: "Meet me at Bezek. Anyone who does not come will have his ox cut in pieces like this bloody piece of ox you see." Thousands and thousands of men hurried to Bezek, until Saul had an army of 330,000 men. Jabesh-Gilead would have help!

Saul sent the messengers from Jabesh-Gilead back with a promise: "By tomorrow when the sun is hot, help will come and you will be saved." Joy filled the city. To keep Saul's plans secret, they said to the Ammonites, "Tomorrow when the sun is hot, we will come out to you." That night Saul divided his army into three parts and crossed the Jordan River. While the Ammonites were still sleeping, just before morning, Saul and his men attacked them, slaughtering them the way you step on ants to kill them. Those who escaped ran every which way, no two together. So, when the sun was hot, just as they had said, the men of Jabesh-Gilead came out of their city. They were saved. For years thereafter they told their children how King Saul had saved their eyes and their city.

Some bad men now said, "Where are the people who mocked King Saul and said, 'How can he be king?' Let's kill them." But Saul said, "No one will be put to death today. God has rescued Israel." Kings should be generous and Saul was generous.

Finally, the old prophet and judge Samuel said, "Come to Gilgal here in the Jordan Valley." All Israel gathered at Gilgal and agreed that Saul was king. His sudden victory over the Ammonites proved it. Saul was KING! He was everything Israel hoped for, tall, commanding, and best of all, brave and cunning against Israel's enemies. Here was a man with the wit and strength to rule! Everyone celebrated.

By and by, Saul left following the LORD, and so the LORD left Saul. After Saul's final battle against the Philistine who lived to the west of Israel, the victorious Philistines found his dead body on the battlefield. They cut off his head and fastened his body to the wall of Beth Shan, a city right in the middle of Israel. When news of this humiliation of Saul arrived in Jabesh-Gilead, the young men of the city showed their own chutzpah. Immediately they marched all night, down the hills to the Jordan River, crossed it, and climbed the steep hills to Beth Shan. They took down Saul's body and burned his body and took Saul's bones back to Jabesh-Gilead to bury properly. Then the people fasted for seven days to remember Saul who had saved their city. King Saul had promised their fathers, "Tomorrow you will be saved," and now in honor of his saving their fathers, the sons risked their lives to bury King Saul, a mighty man, Israel's first king.

Paul the Old Man

"May I Speak to the Mob?"

Acts 21:15 – 22:30

This is a story about an old man almost beaten to death by a mob, arrested by Roman soldiers, and then carried up the steps to a Roman fortress. This is a story about an old man who at that very moment had the chutzpah to ask the Roman commander, "May I speak to the people?" The man's name is Paul.

Paul was used to being arrested, as he was in Philippi and Athens. In Lystra he was mobbed. In Philippi he was flogged and imprisoned. Many times, enemies ran him out of town. For twenty years he traveled through land we now call Turkey and Greece to announce that Jesus of Nazareth was the promised Jewish Messiah. Jesus had come for everyone, both Jew and non-Jew. He would give eternal life to everyone who believed in him and judge all who rejected him. Paul's message made many Gentiles angry. His preaching to Gentiles made Jews furious, especially in Jerusalem.

Why did Paul go to Jerusalem? He had stayed away for twenty years. Now, on the way to Jerusalem, Paul's friends begged him not to go. Agabus, a prophet from Jerusalem, came out to meet him when Paul got close. He took Paul's belt, tied his own hands and feet with it, and prophesied: "Like this, the owner of this belt will be tied up in Jerusalem." Paul said stubbornly, "I am ready to be arrested in Jerusalem and also to die there if necessary for the name of the Lord Jesus." So his friends let him go. Why did Paul go?

Paul wanted to go to Rome. But before he went there, he wanted to see Jerusalem and the Temple one last time. Even more, he wanted to bring a gift of money from the new Gentile churches to the church in Jerusalem.

Paul's arrival scared the Christian church in Jerusalem. Its leaders said to him, "People have heard that you speak against the Temple and against Moses' Law. Here is what you should do to show you are a loyal Jew. Go to the Temple and pay the expenses of four men who have taken vows. That will prove that what people have heard about you is false."

So for seven days Paul went with the four men to the Temple. On the last day, a Jew from the Roman province where Ephesus was saw him. He shouted, "Men of Israel, help! Here is the man who goes everywhere preaching against us, against Moses' law, and against the Temple. And he has brought a Gentile into the Temple itself. He has defiled this holy place!" Paul's accuser had seen him in Jerusalem with a believer from Ephesus named Trophimus, but Paul never brought Trophmus into the Temple. Never mind. The mob believed the shout. They grabbed Paul, dragged him out of the Temple, shut its doors, and began to beat him to death. Roman soldiers rushed into the mob and arrested Paul for causing a riot. They put chains on him.

The Roman commander asked the mob, "Okay. Who is this man? What has he done?" But it was a mob. Everyone shouted at once, and the commander could not make heads or tails of what they screamed. So he ordered his soldiers to take Paul into the nearby Roman fort. When they got to the steps up to the fort, the mob went wild, and the soldiers had to carry Paul on their shoulders. "Kill him. Kill him now," they shouted.

At the top of the stairs, Paul saw what could be his biggest Jewish audience ever! Seizing the moment, he said to the commander in Greek, "May I talk with you?" Surprised, the commander replied, "You speak Greek, do you? Then you are not that Egyptian fellow who led 4,000 men into the wilderness to start a rebellion?" "No," said Paul, "I am a Jew born in Tarsus in Cilicia, a citizen of an important city. May I please speak to the people?" The commander said okay. Maybe by letting Paul speak, he would learn what was going on. But he didn't, because now Paul spoke in Hebrew.

From the top of the stairs, Paul waved his hand for silence. The crowd quieted. Paul began. "My fellow Jews. Listen to my defense." When they heard Paul speak in Hebrew, they got still quieter. "I am a Jew born in Tarsus but educated here, in Jerusalem. My teacher was the famous rabbi Gamaliel who gave me strict instruction in the Law of Moses. I was as dedicated to God as you all are today. Therefore, I persecuted the people who follow this Way – that is what Christians were first called, "Followers of the Way" -- and arrested men and women who followed it. The High Priest and the Council can tell you I'm telling the truth. They gave me letters to take to Damascus to arrest any followers of this Way I found there and bring them here in chains. As we got close to Damascus, a sudden bright light in the middle of the day, brighter than the sun, flashed around me, and I fell to the ground. A voice spoke. 'Saul, Saul – he only began to be called Paul later -- why are you persecuting me?' 'What do you want me to do, Lord?' I asked. The Lord answered me, 'Go to Damascus where a man named Ananias will tell you what to do.'"

The crowd listened, spellbound. Paul continued. "When I got to Damascus, I was blind. After several days, a man named Ananias came and said, 'Brother Saul, see again.' Something like scales fell from my eyes, and I could see. Ananias said, 'The God of our ancestors has chosen you to see his righteous Servant and to hear him speak to you. Now you will be a witness for him to tell everyone what you have seen and heard.' I was baptized. For several years I studied in the wilderness. Then I came back to Jerusalem. While praying in the Temple, I had a vision in which the Lord said to me, 'The Jews here won't listen to you. Go far away to other nations.'"

When Paul said "other nations," the mob erupted in fury. They waved their clothes, threw dust in the air, and shouted for Paul to be killed. The Roman commander, not knowing what Paul had said to make the crowd go wild, ordered Paul taken into the fort and whipped. They tied Paul to a pole and ripped off his clothes to flog him. A soldier lifted his arm with a whip. At the last moment, Paul said to the watching officer, "Is it according to the law for you to whip a Roman citizen who hasn't even been on trial yet?" The soldier's hand stayed in the air. The officer hurried to the commander. "Watch out," he said. "This man is a Roman citizen."

The commander came to Paul. "You are a Roman citizen, are you? So am I, and it cost me a lot of money." How could Paul have had enough money to buy Roman citizenship, he thought. Paul answered, "But I am a Roman by birth." Immediately, the men about to whip Paul drew back and the commander was afraid.

Paul stayed in prison for the next several years, first in Jerusalem, then in the port city of Caesarea. He spoke to governors and kings about Jesus. When Paul spoke to the new Roman governor Festus, along with the Jewish King Agrippa and his sister Berenice, Governor Festus suddenly interrupted him. "Paul, you are crazy!" Paul answered, "No, most noble Festus. I am not crazy. You can ask King Agrippa. He knows all about these things concerning Jesus. Nothing was done in secret. King Agrippa, you believe the prophets, don't you?" Agrippa answered, "You almost convince me to be a Christian." Paul replied, "I wish you and everyone who hears me would be like me – except for these chains, of course." In the end Governor Festus sent Paul to Rome at Paul's request, to have Caesar judge him.

Paul's preaching to an angry mob at the Temple got him to Rome. While a prisoner in Rome he got close to Caesar's family. Soon he wrote to Christians in the Roman colony of Philippi, "Those from Caesar's household say hello."

Where will godly chutzpah lead you? Only God knows. Paul's chutzpah got him to Rome for free – but as a prisoner! If you live with wit and courage, you won't know before things happen how they will turn out, but your Father in heaven knows, and he always cares for you.

Rahab the Outcast

"Your God Rules Heaven and Earth"

Joshua 2, 6:17-27

R ahab was not a respectable woman. She owned a house on the wall of the very old city of Jericho close to the Jordan River. It was just north of the Dead Sea, on the road to the mountains of Canaan. Any man could go to Rahab's house day or night to spend time with her for money, no questions asked. That was how she made her living.

Like everyone else in Jericho Rahab was afraid of Israel. They were camped on the other side of the Jordan River, right across from Jericho. Jericho was next!

One evening towards dusk two men came to her house. They were spies sent by Joshua to see Jericho's defenses and the mood of its people. Were they afraid or confident? The men went to Rahab's house because everyone expected men to go to her house. Rahab knew these two men were spies from Joshua and she had sudden hope for herself and her family. Her plan would take courage. She would protect them if they would promise not to kill her and her relatives. Naturally, if Jericho's rulers found out what she was doing, they would kill her. Rahab would act alone in order to escape the City of Destruction and join Israel.

Someone saw the spies go into Rahab's house and told the city leaders. They ordered her: -- "Bring out those men who went into your house. They have come to spy out our land." Rahab lied. "Some men came to my house, but I did not know where they came from. They left before our city's gates were shut at sundown. Quick, send men after them to catch them before they escape. They can't have gone far and you will catch them."

Immediately, Rahab took the two spies to the flat roof of her house. (In Jericho it never snows because it is more than eight hundred feet below sea level, so all the roofs are flat.) On the roof Rahab had stalks of flax laid out to dry so that she could later make cloth from them. She hid the spies under the stalks of flax. Meanwhile, the men of Jericho chased the phantom spies all the way to the Jordan River, but they did not catch them because they were still on Rahab's roof!

After the messengers from the king had gone, Rahab told the spies why she was helping them, calling Israel's God by his special name, the LORD. "I know that the LORD has given you this land. Everyone in the country is terrified of you. We have heard how the LORD dried up the Red Sea in front of you when you were leaving Egypt. We have also heard how you killed Sihon and Og, the two Amorite kings east of the Jordan. We were afraid as soon as we heard about it; we have lost our courage because of you. The LORD your God is God in heaven above and here on earth (Joshua 2:9-12)" Rahab's words were her statement of faith. She believed that the LORD, the God of Israel, is the true God, ruler of heaven and earth. God counted her faith in Him as righteousness.

Rahab told the spies what she wanted for her help. "Swear to me by the LORD. Since I have shown you kindness, you also please show kindness to my father's house. Give me proof that you will do this. Then you will save alive my father, and my mother, and my brothers, and my sisters, and all that they have, and save our lives from death."

The men answered, "Our life for yours, as long as you tell no one about our business here. Then, when the LORD gives us the land, we will deal kindly with you." Rahab let them down in the dark from her house on the wall to the ground outside. She said, "Run to the mountains and stay there for three days until they give up hunting for you. After that you can go on your way."

The men answered, "When we come to the land, put a red cord in the window you let us down from. We will be blameless for breaking our oath to you if you don't follow our directions. Gather your father and mother and brothers and sisters and their whole household into your house. Make them stay there. Whoever leaves your house will be killed, and their blood will not be our fault." Rahab answered, "I will do what you say."

The spies ran to the hills and hid for three days. Then they went back and reported to Joshua everything they had seen and heard and about the oath they had sworn to Rahab. Meanwhile, all Jericho, including Rahab and her relatives, sat behind their walls with the gates closed and waited in fear.

God worked things out as Rahab planned. Israel conquered Jericho. They let Rahab and her relatives live. Later Rahab married an Israelite from the tribe of Judah named Salmon. They had a son named Boaz who married Ruth. Their son Obed was the father of Jesse, who was the father of David, the greatest king of Israel. In the first chapter of the New Testament, Matthew includes Rahab by name as an ancestor of Jesus.

Far from being silent about Rahab's work as an outcast, the Bible emphasizes it to show that God saves even unrespectable people who trust in him. The writer of the letter to the Hebrews includes Rahab as a hero of faith. "It was faith that kept the prostitute Rahab from being killed with those who disobeyed God, for she gave the Israelite spies a friendly welcome (Hebrews 11:31)."

A Lame Man and his Friends

"Let's Rip Up the Roof"

Mark 2:1-12, Luke 5:17-26

Once there was a man who was lame. He could not walk. We don't know his name or why he was lame. Maybe he was born lame. Maybe he had an accident. In any case, he depended on friends to carry him around on a homemade stretcher. In those days, there were no wheelchairs or handicapped access ramps. He never expected to walk again.

The lame man lived in the trading town of Capernaum on the north shore of the Sea of Galilee. Interesting things didn't happen there. Sudden storms might sweep down from the hills. Fishermen brought their boats in each morning with many fish or none. Nearby Roman soldiers kept the peace, guaranteed the value of their coins, made sure people paid taxes, and appeared often enough to annoy people. Any excitement had to do with three annual trips south to Jerusalem for feasts, or about who just died or got married or had a baby. Every now and then someone tried to start a war against Rome. Mostly it was a dull life, especially for people who were lame.

One day something totally new happened. The teacher from the nearby village of Nazareth settled in Capernaum with his disciples. His name was Jesus. He preached a thrilling message: "The Kingdom of God is near. Repent and believe this Announcement." People ran to hear him, especially because he healed sick, blind, and lame people. Evil spirits were afraid of him and obeyed his commands.

Returning from a trip to villages near Capernaum one day, Jesus moved back into the house he stayed in. It had a flat roof, a garden next to it, and a door to the street in the wall surrounding the house and garden. Here was the lame man's chance. All he had to do was get to Jesus and ask. But many people got there first and crowded into the room where Jesus sat and out into the garden. When his friends brought the lame man on his mat, the crowd would not let them in to see Jesus. So the lame man and his friends thought of something that took a lot of chutzpah.

His friends carried the lame man up to the roof right above where Jesus sat. The roof was made of poles and tightly woven matting to keep rain out. Why were they on the roof? To tear a hole in it and lower the lame man to Jesus. They began taking the roof apart. Pieces fell down. People shouted, "Stop!" They went right on until they could lower the lame man on his mat to Jesus. Down through the air he came.

People were surprised and more than annoyed by their chutzpah. Then Jesus said something totally surprising. Seeing the faith of these men, even to the point of seeming crazy, he said to the lame man, "My son, your sins are forgiven you." What sins? We don't know. Everyone has committed sins against God and neighbor that need to be forgiven.

Bible teachers in the crowd were shocked. "Who can forgive sins except God alone?" they thought. Jesus, knowing what they were thinking, asked a question. "Is it easier to say to a lame man, 'Get up and walk,' or to say, 'Your sins are forgiven?' But so you will know that the Son of Man has authority on earth to forgive sins" – and then Jesus turned to the lame man and said, "Get up, pick up your mat, and walk home." The lame man stood up, picked up his mat, made his way through the crowd, and walked home. "Wow," everyone said. "We've never seen anything like this before." Amazed, they praised God. What a story to tell their families and neighbors!

The Bible teachers had nothing to say to Jesus' question. Who could tell whether God has forgiven sins or not? But everyone could see a lame man walk. And walk he did!

Another thing Jesus said gave the Bible teachers something to think about. He called himself "the Son of Man." What did that mean? The Bible teachers probably knew where that title came from. It's from a vision God gave to the prophet Daniel. In the vision one "like a Son of Man" came to the Ancient of Days, in other words, to God himself. The Son of Man would be given an everlasting kingdom that would never be destroyed (Daniel 7:13-14). When Jesus called himself "the Son of Man" it meant that he was claiming to be the promised Messiah who would be King of Israel with authority to forgive sins!

When Jesus forgave the lame man's sin, calling himself the "Son of Man," he meant that the Kingdom of God was near because he, Jesus, had come. He had God's authority because he was actually God himself, and God backed him up by giving him the power to heal the lame man. The Bible teachers were right, of course. Only God can forgive sins, and Jesus is God. Jesus forgave the sins of this lame man because he – and his friends -- had faith to tear up a roof to get to Jesus. They knew he could heal him, and he did even more. He forgave his sins.

Ruth the Foreigner

"Marry Me"

Book of Ruth

Ruth was a young widow from Moab who had the chutzpah to ask a rich, older man to marry her. He did. This is her story. The Moabite Ruth first married Chilion, a young Israelite. Chilion's father Elimelech moved his family to Moab because there was a famine in Bethlehem. Chilion's brother Mahlon married Orpah, also a Moabite. Then all three men died, Elimelech, Chilion, and Mahlon. Ruth, Orpah, and their mother-in-law Naomi were now widows.

When Naomi heard that Bethlehem had food again, she decided to go home. She said to her daughters-in-law, "Go back to your families. I have no more sons for you to marry." In Israel the brother of a man who died with no children had to marry the brother's widow. Orpah went home, but Ruth now worshiped the LORD, the God of Israel, not Chemosh, the evil god of Moab. Ruth refused to leave Naomi. She said to her, "Don't ask me to leave you! Wherever you go, I will go; wherever you live, I will live. Your people will be my people, and your God will be my God. Wherever you die, I will die, and that is where I will be buried. May the LORD's worst punishment come upon me if I let anything but death separate me from you (Ruth 1:16-17)." So Naomi and Ruth walked on to

Bethlehem. They got there as the April barley harvest began. They moved into Elimelech's old house, but what were they going to eat?

Ruth said to Naomi, "May I go into the fields to glean?" Gleaning means to pick up the barley stalks the reapers leave behind. "Go ahead," said Naomi. She was feeling so sorry for herself she could not think what to do. "I left here with a husband and two sons, and now I come home with nothing," she told Bethlehem's women. "Don't call me Naomi. Call me 'Bitter.'"

Ruth left their house and walked alone out of Bethlehem looking for somewhere to glean food. She happened on a field where men were harvesting the ripe barley. Ruth began gleaning. Soon the field's owner, Boaz, came by. "The LORD be with you," he saluted his workers. "The LORD be with you," they answered. Boaz noticed Ruth. "Who is that young woman?" "She is the foreigner who just came back with Naomi," his foreman replied. Boaz went to Ruth, who had stopped to rest in some shade. "Do what I say. Stay in my fields and follow the other young women. My men will leave you alone. When you get thirsty, get water from our water jugs." "Why are you being so kind to me, a foreigner?" Ruth asked. Boaz answered, "I have heard about you and how you showed loyalty to your mother-in-law and came to live among a new people. May the God of Israel reward you! "

At mealtime, Boaz invited Ruth to eat with him and his men. He passed some roasted grain to her, so much that she got full and had grain left over to take home. Boaz then ordered his workers. "Let her glean wherever she wants to. Pull out some extra stalks from the sheaves and leave them for her."

What a great story Boaz' workers had that night. Rich Boaz was interested in a young woman! The workers and soon the whole village went over the details of that day in the field. He fed her. He told his workers to leave extra stalks of barley for her. He told her to come back. Did Boaz really like Ruth? Would she like him, an older man? He was rich, of course.

Naomi asked Ruth where she went that day. "To a field belonging to a man named Boaz." Instantly, Naomi had an idea. "Boaz is a kinsman-redeemer, a close relative of ours. By our law he has the right to buy the land my dead husband sold when we went to Moab. Stay in Boaz's field! Don't go anywhere else."

Weeks passed. Barley harvest ended and wheat harvest began. Every day, Ruth went to Boaz's fields, ate with him and his workers at noontime, and came home with enough food for both her and Naomi. The town continued talking. "Would rich Boaz finally marry? Would he ever get up the nerve to ask her? Would a young woman like Ruth even want him?"

Threshing time began for both the barley and wheat harvests. The men beat the stalks of grain, threw it in the air with wooden shovels so the wind could blow the chaff away and leave just the grain. Naomi thought it was time for Ruth to suggest marriage to Boaz. However, she had to do it in private to avoid possible humiliation, and there was a problem. People don't have much privacy in villages.

Naomi had a plan that required a lot of chutzpah. She told Ruth, "Wash yourself, put on your best clothes and some perfume. Go where Boaz is threshing barley after it is too dark for people to tell you are a woman. See where he lies down after eating and drinking. Then lie down silently by him in the dark. He will tell you what to do."

Brave Ruth agreed to do this crazy thing. What if she were caught? What would Boaz do when he found her there? Would he shout, "You can't be here. You are a woman." What would Boaz say? Ruth washed, put on her best clothes, which probably weren't much good, added some perfume, and waited until dark. Then she went to the threshing floor and lay down by Boaz. The danger, if someone else saw her, was utter disgrace. Women did not belong there.

Boaz rolled over in his sleep. He bumped into Ruth. "Who are you?" he whispered, startled awake. "I am Ruth," she whispered back. "Because you are Naomi's kinsman-redeemer, you should take care of us. Please spread your cloak over me," by which she meant, "Marry me." Shy Boaz understood and was delighted. Still whispering, he said, "May the LORD bless you. What great family loyalty you have. You could have gone after another man, a young one. I will do what you ask. Everyone in town knows you are a good woman."

Why did Boaz say everyone knew Ruth was a good woman? Because there are easier ways for a pretty young widow to get food than by gleaning, but not good ways, and Ruth had not taken them. Day after day, all Bethlehem watched Ruth leave their village at daybreak. Then they saw her come back at dusk with a little grain after yet another hot day of back-breaking labor in the sun. Yes, everyone knew Ruth was a good woman.

Boaz continued, "Tomorrow, I will ask the relative who is more closely related to Elimelech than I am if he wants to buy back his field. If he says no, the responsibility will be mine. Now stay until morning dawns and then go. It should not be known that a woman was here all night." As light appeared in the east, Boaz put a huge amount of grain into Ruth's cloak. She went home and told everything to her mother-in-law Naomi, who had not slept all night. Naomi said, "Now wait. Boaz will take care of this today." Naomi knew men. After all, she had been married to a man and had two sons.

Boaz sat down in the gate, where men did business in those days. He gathered ten witnesses and then waited for the closer relative to Elimelech to come by. "Sit here my friend. You are Elimelech's closest relative. Do you want to buy back his field?" "Yes, indeed," said the relative. Then Boaz followed Naomi's lead, combining two laws in Israel, marry your dead brother's widow and buy back family land. "Of course, if you buy the field, then you must also marry Ruth." When Boaz named Ruth, the closer relative quickly said no thanks. He mumbled something about the awkward-ness of his children's inheritance. Why make rich Boaz angry by taking Ruth? Everyone knew he liked her. "You buy back the field," he said.

So Boaz married Ruth. Everyone was happy. "May Ruth be like Leah and Rachel who built up Jacob's family with many sons. And may she be like Tamar who built up Judah's family with a son named Perez," they said. (Tamar was a Canaanite widow of two of Judah's three sons, and she too had daring, maybe even more than Ruth had, but that is another story.)

In due time, Ruth had a son named Obed. The women said to Naomi, "Now you have a grandson to make you feel young again and to take care of you in your old age." It wasn't long before Boaz, or Ruth, or both of them, told the story of their unusual love affair and that is how we know about it. Later Obed had a son named Jesse, who had eight sons. His youngest, David, kept sheep, played a harp, wrote Psalms, killed a giant, and became king. Ruth, Boaz, Obed, Jesse, and David, are all ancestors of Jesus Christ, the elder brother of all Christians. Jesus saved us from slavery to sin so we could be adopted as sons of God. He is our Kinsman-Redeemer and also the Bridegroom of the Church, mother of God's adopted children. At the Resurrection, we will meet Jesus face to face, and probably his resourceful and courageous ancestor Ruth too.

Daniel the Young Captive

"Please Feed Us Only Vegetables"

Daniel 1

Only the Christ's Kingdom is forever. No country lives forever, not even the iron empire of Rome. Its final years were messy, as are the final years of every nation whose time is up. So it was for the Kingdom of Judah where Daniel lived when he was a child. Over a period of sixteen years, Nebuchadnezzar the Chaldean invaded Judah three times, 605 B.C., 598 B.C., and 589 B.C. Each time he took people back to Babylon. Daniel went with the first group of prisoners in 605 B.C.

Along with Daniel went many other young men from the royal family. They had to be healthy, handsome, and well educated. With Babylonian soldiers herding them along, they walked 800 miles, north, then east, and then south to Babylon along the Euphrates River.

Why did King Nebuchadnezzar want these young men? They were going to help him rule his growing empire. Without parents or family, or children to nurture, or a country to defend, they would be totally dedicated to serving him. Stuck in Babylon, they would also be hostages for good behavior by the new king of Judah whom Nebuchadnezzar put on the throne.

Even in the worst of situations, God rarely leaves his people completely by themselves. Daniel had three like-minded friends who had been given new Babylonian names. We know them by those new names, Shadrach, Meshach, and Abednego. Daniel's new Babylonian name was Belteshazzar, but we know him by his Jewish name, Daniel. Together with the young men, these four Jewish teenage boys had to learn the Babylonian language, its literature, and its statecraft. They already knew Jewish literature and statecraft, especially the Law of Moses. In a foreign land, with no hope of going home, would Daniel and his friends stay loyal to the God of Israel?

Nebuchadnezzar ordered his school principal, the eunuch Ashpenaz, to feed his new pupils the same food and wine his court ate, plenty of it, and well prepared. However, the Law of God did not allow Israelites to eat certain foods commonly eaten by other nations. Most famously, they were not allowed to eat any part of a pig: no bacon, no ham, no pork chops, not even a pig's ears or tail. When they ate other meat from other animals, they had to be killed in a certain precise way. There were many other food rules as well. Would Daniel and his three friends disobey God's Law and eat these forbidden foods that were part of the King's diet?

Very politely, the captive teenager Daniel went to Ashpenaz and asked, "May we eat different food, please?" Ashpenaz liked Daniel, but he was afraid to agree. He said, "I am afraid of my lord the king. Your food comes by his personal orders. What if he sees that you are in worse condition than all the other young men your age? You will endanger my head if you don't eat what I was ordered to feed you."

Daniel did not give up. He went to Ashpenaz' servant who actually gave them their food. He made a proposal. "Feed us just vegetables and fruit and only water to drink. After ten days see how we look. Then decide what food you will feed us." Ashpenaz' servant also liked Daniel and bravely agreed to Daniel's request for a vegetarian diet. It was a scientific experiment. Daniel and his friends were the experimental group fed a new vegetarian diet. The other young men were the control group fed the original diet of rich food and wine. How would Daniel and his friends look after ten days of a vegetarian diet compared to the other students?

When the ten days of the experiment were finished, Ashpenaz' servant looked at Daniel and his three friends closely. What did he see? By God's kindness, they looked healthier than the other captive students who ate the King's food. So Daniel and his friends were allowed to continue eating food that Jews were allowed to eat. The other students probably did not complain, because how many young men want to eat vegetarian?

After three years in school, King Nebuchadnezzar examined his captive pupils who would run his Empire for him. Daniel finished first. See how God rewarded him for his faithfulness? After Daniel began his career working for the King, he got lots of promotions and had lots of adventures for the next sixty years. He even worked as an old man for the Persians who conquered the Babylonians. The Persian king Darius put him in a lion's den all night because of a plot by jealous rivals. But that is another story for another time.

Abigail, a Fool's Wife

"Please Blame Me"

I Samuel 25

A bigail was smart, beautiful, and wise. Her husband Nabal was
stupid and mean -- but he was rich. He had 3000 sheep and 1000
goats. They lived near the town of Carmel far in the south of Judah on
land inherited from Caleb, Moses' faithful spy centuries before. The hill-
side sloping down from the mountains of Israel to the desert of Arabia
had two springs on it. It didn't rain much there, but the springs provided
water for Nabal's flocks.

Suddenly one morning, ten men showed up. They came from David,
God's second anointed king after King Saul. David was hiding among
the hills to escape from jealous King Saul who wanted to kill him. It was
springtime, the time of year when sheep get sheared, that is, their wool
gets cut off. Sheep-shearing was always a happy time of year and it ended
with feasting and joy. "We come from David," the men said to Nabal.
Everyone in Israel knew who David was, so they did not need to explain
more. "He wishes you and your family well," the men said. "He has heard
you are shearing your sheep. He has been good to your shepherds. Just
ask them. We never took anything from them. Please share some of the
food that God has given you."

The men were speaking to Abigail's stupid and mean husband, and they got a stupid and mean answer. Nabal said, "Not a chance." Then he got insulting. "Who is David? Never heard of him. Nowadays people often run away from their masters. I'm not going to take the grain and the slaughtered sheep from my men and give it to you. Be off! Go away!" The ten men returned to David and told him why they came back with nothing. "We were polite, but he said no." They told David how Nabal had spoken to them and insulted him. David flew into a fury and said to his men, "Put on your swords."

Meanwhile, Nabal's scared servants went to Nabal's wife, Abigail. "Have you heard? David sent some messengers to our master, and he insulted them. But they were very good to us and never stole anything. In fact, they protected us night and day. Please, think fast what to do. We can't talk to Nabal. He won't listen to anyone." In an instant, Abigail knew that their lives were in danger. David was a soldier. He had a small army, and he would likely be on his way for revenge. With decisive planning, Abigail acted immediately. Of course, she was acting contrary to what her husband wanted, but the situation demanded it.

Abigail ordered the servants to gather food for David's men. How much food? A LOT! Two hundred loaves of bread, several bags full of wine, five roasted sheep, thirty-five pounds of roasted grain, a hundred cakes of raisins, two hundred cakes of figs, all loaded quickly on donkeys. Abigail sent the servants with the food ahead and she followed behind. She did not tell Nabal what she was doing.

Abigail was riding her donkey on the path around a bend when suddenly she met David. David had been thinking about how Nabal was repaying him evil for good. "May God strike me dead if I don't kill every one of the men and boys," he said to himself.

When Abigail saw David, she got off her donkey and fell to the ground in front of David. "Please, sir, listen to me! Let me take the blame. Please, don't pay attention to Nabal, that good for nothing. He is exactly what his name means – a fool (I Samuel 25:24-25)." Abigail continued, "Please, sir, accept this present I have brought you, and give it to your men (I

Samuel 25:27)." Both Abigail and Nabal knew the politics in Israel, how David had killed Goliath, married the king's daughter, and then Saul had turned against him in a jealous rage. Abigail went on, "The LORD will make you king, and your descendants also, because you are fighting his battles; and you will not do anything evil as long as you live (I Samuel 25:28)." "When the LORD has done all the good things he has promised you and has made you king of Israel, then you will not have to feel regret or remorse, sir, for having killed without cause or for taking your own revenge. And when the LORD has blessed you, sir, please do not forget me (I Samuel 25:30-31)."

The huge gift impressed David. This smart, beautiful, and humble woman pleased him. He knew his plans for murder and revenge were wrong. He said to Abigail, "Thank God for your good sense and for keeping me from murder. The LORD sent you. If you had not come, all of Nabal's men would have been dead by morning." So David accepted the gift and went back to the hills. Abigail and her servants rode home.

When Abigail got home, she found Nabal eating a huge feast. He was drunk, so she did not tell him what she had done or how she had met David coming to kill them. The next morning when he was sober, Abigail told him everything. Whether from anger or fear at what might have happened we do not know, but Nabal had a sudden paralyzing stroke. It was from God. Ten days later he died.

When David heard Nabal was dead, he said, "Good. Praise the LORD. He has taken revenge on Nabal for insulting me and has kept me from doing wrong." Then he sent some servants to Carmel to say to Abigail, "David sent us to bring you back to be his wife." Abigail bowed low and said, "I am his servant, ready to wash the feet of his servants." This was her respectful way of saying, "Yes." She got ready quickly and took five maids with her and became David's wife. Her boldness and quick thinking saved the lives of her family and then made her the wife of King David.

A Canaanite Mother

"Even Dogs Get to Eat the Scraps"

Matthew 15:21-28, Mark 7:24-30

Jesus and his disciples walked out of Galilee to the north. They would get away from arguing with Pharisees for a time. They went to Tyre and rented a house. Tyre was an old Phoenician city where Canaanites lived. But even there everyone knew about Jesus. Soon, a desperate Canaanite woman heard they were there and barged in on these thirteen men.

She fell at Jesus' feet and begged, "Son of David, have mercy on me. An evil spirit is in my daughter and she is in a terrible condition." Jesus said nothing. He went on eating. His disciples couldn't stand the noise she was making. They told Jesus, "Send her away." Still, Jesus said nothing. The woman went on. "Son of David, have mercy on me."

Finally Jesus spoke to her. "I have been sent to the lost sheep of Israel." This woman was NOT one of the lost sheep of Israel. She was a Canaanite. Did she have any right to ask the Jewish Messiah, the Son of David, for help? No. She already knew this, of course. When she called Jesus the "Son of David," she showed that she knew Jesus was the Jewish Savior.

This woman also knew something else. She was a woman among thirteen men with muscles. Jesus was a carpenter, and at least four disciples were fishermen. They could easily pick her up and throw her out the door. They had certainly not invited her into the house to interrupt their meal.

But this unnamed woman was desperate, and she had chutzpah. She was ready to take the consequences for the trouble she was making because she knew Jesus had authority and power over evil spirits. He could help her.

No one came with this Canaanite woman. She had no friends to help her. Blind Bartimaeus had a blind beggar friend; Daniel had three friends; David had a whole army rooting for him. This woman was alone like Rahab had once been alone, part of the descendants of cursed Canaan. But she would NOT be put off.

She continued begging, saying over and over "Help me, sir!" Jesus said no again! "It is not right to take the children's food and throw it to dogs." The Jews sometimes called people like her "dogs." They wouldn't even eat with Gentiles, let alone Canaanite Gentiles. In those days, dogs were not house pets. They roamed the streets and ate dead things. They were dangerous pests. To call someone a dog was very insulting.

Still this woman persisted. She saw her position perfectly and accepted it: Jews come first. It was what Paul wrote later. The saving work of Jesus is for the Jews first (Romans 1:16).

What should this Canaanite mother do? Give up? The disciples wanted her shoved out the door. Jesus said he came for the Jews. He called her a dog. What should she do? Act insulted? No. She gave Jesus a humble and logical answer.

"That's true, sir. But don't dogs get to eat scraps of food dropped from the table?" Wasn't that a clever answer! Even today, children sometimes feed pet dogs under the table with food they don't want. Maybe you have done that. Now what would Jesus say to her? It was true! Dogs get to eat scraps of food dropped from a table.

Jesus saw her desperate love for her daughter. He saw her unyielding faith in him. He saw her chutzpah. Finally, Jesus said what she wanted to hear. "You are a woman of great faith. What you want will be done for you." That was all she wanted to hear. She did not need Jesus to come with her. She knew Jesus only had to say the word, and her daughter would be healed. So she left the thirteen men in the house and went home. When she got there, she found her daughter well and in her right mind.

Jael a Blessed Woman

"Come in and Rest"

Judges 4-5

J ael was the wife of Heber the Kenite. They lived in a tent and kept
sheep and goats in the days when judges ruled Israel. The Kenites were
part of the tribe Moses' wife came from near Mount Sinai, but Heber's
family had moved far north to live near the Sea of Galilee.

When Jael got up from her sleeping mat one morning, she knew what
would happen that day. There would be a battle between Sisera's army
and Barak's army. That hardly concerned her or her husband. They were
at peace with Sisera's city, Hazor, and also at peace with Israel. However,
she knew that battles usually hurt many people nearby as scared soldiers
ran here and there, so she stayed alert all day watching.

The battle came about this way. Hazor had been stealing food from
the Israelite people who lived nearby. Finally, God told the prophetess
Deborah to tell an Israelite named Barak, "Gather an army and go fight
Sisera. I will make sure you win." In spite of God's promise of victory,
Barak was afraid. He said to Deborah, "Okay, I'll go, but only if you
come with me." Deborah answered, "Alright, I will come. But the honor
of killing Sisera will go to a woman, not to you or any other man."

Barak gathered an army of 10,000 out of Israel's northern tribes, Zebulon and Naphtali, and headed towards Sisera's city. Deborah went with him. Sisera heard about it and got 900 iron chariots and all his men to go fight Barak. Deborah encouraged Barak: "Go. The LORD is leading you. Attack and you will defeat Sisera." So Barak and his men charged down from Mount Tabor and attacked Sisera and his army. God threw Sisera's chariots and men into confusion and they were soon running everywhere, just as Jael knew happens after battles. Sisera himself got down from his chariot and ran for his life.

When Sisera could run no more, he came to Jael's tent. She was standing by the door, looking and listening. "Come in," she invited. "Come in and rest. Don't be afraid." Jael knew who Sisera was. Everyone who lived near Sisera's city, Hazor, knew who he was. Sisera came in and lay down. He was very, very tired. Jael thoughtfully covered him with a cloak.

"Give me some water to drink," he said. "I am thirsty." So Jael poured a bowl of goat's milk and gave him a drink. She knew that milk would help him fall asleep. Sisera told her, "Now stand in the door of the tent, and if anyone comes by, say, 'No one's here except me.'" Then Sisera fell into the deep sleep of exhaustion.

Jael waited until Sisera was sound asleep. Then she took a tent peg in one hand and a hammer in the other. Softly, she crept to sleeping Sisera, still dangerous because he was a great warrior even though he was sound asleep. What if he heard her? Putting the tent peg gently in front of Sisera's ear at his temple where the bone is soft, Jael suddenly hammered the peg with all her might. The peg went through Sisera's head into the ground. He died instantly.

Soon Barak and his men came by, still chasing Sisera. "Come here," Jael said. "See what is in my tent. I will show you the man you are looking for." When Barak came into the tent, he saw General Sisera dead, a nail through his temples holding his head fast to the ground.

Later, Deborah composed a song about the battle, praising Jael, not Barak, as the hero.

The most fortunate of women is Jael, the wife of Heber the Kenite — the most fortunate of women who live in tents. *Sisera asked for water, but she gave him milk; she brought him cream in a beautiful bowl.*

She took a tent peg in one hand, a worker's hammer in the other; she struck Sisera and crushed his skull; she pierced him through the head.

He sank to his knees, fell down and lay still at her feet. At her feet he sank to his knees and fell, he fell to the ground, dead. Sisera's mother looked out of the window; she gazed from behind the lattice. "Why is his chariot so late in coming?" she asked. "Why are his horses so slow to return?"

Her wisest friends answered her, and she told herself over and over, "They are only finding things to capture and divide, a woman or two for every soldier, rich cloth for Sisera, embroidered pieces for the neck of the queen."

So may all your enemies die like that, O LORD, but may your friends shine like the rising sun! (Judges 5:24-31)."

Did Jael expect the general of Hazor's army to come to her tent that day? Lie down in it? Fall asleep in it? Of course not! Only God knew such a thing would happen because he planned it. Jael knew nothing about Deborah's prophecy that the honor of killing Sisera would go to a woman. But Jael had chutzpah and knew what to do with Sisera when opportunity suddenly came. Clever and brave Jael, a favored and blessed woman!

Queen Esther the Brave

"If I Perish, I Perish"

Esther 1 - 10

The Persian Court had a job opening, Queen. Ahasuerus the King, called by the Greeks Xerxes, had fired Queen Vashti. She refused his demand to parade her good looks for some drunken guests to enjoy. Then Xerxes wrote a bombastic letter to every province, saying that wives should obey their husbands. Not long after that, Ahasuerus (Xerxes) tried to conquer Greece and lost, leading to a great deal of boasting by Athens. Things were not going well for Ahasuerus, and he needed cheering up.

Ahasuerus' advisors had an idea: tell the governors to send the most gorgeous young girls to Susa, the capital city, and let the King choose a new Queen. Among the girls rounded up for the Queen Contest was Hadassah, also called Esther. She had a beautiful face and figure. Esther was a cousin of Mordecai, descended from Jews who stayed behind in Persia after King Cyrus let them go home. Mordecai brought Esther up as his own daughter after her parents died. Mordecai said, "Don't tell anyone you are Jewish," so she kept it secret.

The chief eunuch liked Esther and gave her seven women to serve her while she had special treatments and a special diet to make her even more beautiful. (Long ago, eunuchs were a special kind of servant in kings' palaces.) When it was her turn to go to King Ahasuerus, she wore what the chief eunuch advised. It worked. The King liked Esther best out of all the beautiful young women and made her his new Queen. Being Queen meant that Esther had her own palace and her own servants, but she could never leave the palace! She had to use her servants to take messages to and from Mordecai.

Mordecai had a job in the court bureaucracy. One day, after Esther had become Queen, he heard two palace eunuchs plotting to kill the King. He sent a message to Queen Esther about it. She told the King. He investigated and the plotters were executed. The whole affair was written up in the court records, giving Mordecai credit for saving the king's life.

Around this time Ahasuerus promoted a man named Haman to be Prime Minister. This meant that everyone had to bow to Haman when he came to work or went home. Everyone obeyed and bowed low, everyone except Mordecai. Mordecai the Jew was a man with chutzpah, and he refused to bow ritually to a mere man.

Haman could not stand it that even one person refused to bow to him. He plotted revenge. He would kill Mordecai and not only him but all the Jews too. Haman thought how to present his murderous idea to the king. He went to King Ahasuerus and said, "There is a people scattered throughout your empire. They have different customs than ours and do not fit into your kingdom. They should be killed. If you agree, I will pay 375 tons of silver to the treasury." Ahasuerus signed the necessary decree: on the eve of Passover, kill all the Jews. Ahasuerus did not know personally any of these Jews whose death sentence he signed. Or so he thought! He believed Haman that killing them would protect the kingdom.

The Jews in Susa were terrified. Mordecai wore sackcloth on his body and put ashes on his head. He wandered the streets wailing loudly. One of Esther's servants told her what he was doing. Had he gone crazy? She sent new clothes to Mordecai. He refused them. Then she sent a messenger to ask what was wrong since inside the palace she had no idea what Haman had plotted. Mordecai sent back news about the plan to kill all the Jews and asked Esther to plead with King Ahasuerus not to do this evil thing.

Esther answered, "I can't just go to the King whenever I want to. He has not called for me for a month. Anyone who goes to the King without being summoned must die." Mordecai sent another message. "Go anyway. Who knows? Maybe you are Queen for such a time as this! If you don't go, God will save his people another way, but you will certainly die." So Esther sent yet another message: "Gather the Jews of Susa and fast three days for me and pray. Then I will go. If I perish, I perish." Esther had courage. She was also clever. She understood the whole situation, and she saw how she could trap Haman and foil his evil plan.

Once the fasting and prayer finished, Queen Esther, knowing she might be going to her death, put on her royal robes and went to the King. When he saw her, he graciously held out his golden scepter, which meant, "You may come forward." So great was his affection for Esther that he asked, "What do you want? Whatever it is, even half my kingdom, I will give it to you." Esther said, "All I want is this: come to a banquet I will prepare. And bring Haman, your Prime Minister. Then I will tell you what I want." At the banquet, the King asked, "What do you want?" Esther replied, "Only that you and Haman come tomorrow to another banquet, and then I will tell you."

Haman was elated. He had no idea that Esther was Jewish or that Mordecai was related to her. He boasted to his family that he alone had eaten with the King and Queen. Then he remembered Mordecai who still would not bow to him and complained that he would never be happy as long as he had to look at Mordecai. So his considerate wife and friends said, "Build a 75 foot pole in your courtyard to stick Mordecai on. That will make you feel better." Haman built the pole.

That night Ahasuerus could not sleep. Perhaps he had eaten and drunk too much at Queen Esther's feast! He asked his servants to bring him the chronicles of his kingdom and read him to sleep. Hearing about their own greatness often soothes kings and emperors. When they read about how Mordecai had reported the plot to murder him, he asked, "What has been done to reward him?" "Nothing," they answered. Hearing someone enter, he asked, "Who just came in?" "Haman," they said. "Bring him here." "Haman, what should be done for the man whom the king wants to honor?" he asked. Haman thought Ahasuerus meant him, so he thought what he would like. "Put clothes you have worn on him, have him ride a horse the King has ridden, and have a nobleman lead him through the city, crying 'This is how the King honors a man.'" "Good idea," said King Ahasuerus. "Do it for Mordecai. You lead him around." Haman could not believe his ears. What a defeat for him and what honor for his enemy Mordecai! But he had to obey the king and he did it.

When humiliated Haman got back home, he told his wife everything. She was unsympathetic. "It means you are losing power to Mordecai the Jew." Just then, a messenger came to call Haman to Esther's second banquet. At least that was some consolation to Haman. He got to dine with the King and Queen a second time.

After dinner, curious King Ahasuerus asked again, "Esther, what do you want?" She replied, "Only my life. That's all. I, and my people, have been sold to death. If it were just to be sold as slaves, I would have kept quiet and not bothered you, but now we are about to be exterminated." Astonished, Ahasuerus exclaimed, "Who would do such a thing?" "Our enemy is Haman," said the Queen, pointing at him. The furious King walked out into the garden. Terrified, Haman fell at the Queen's couch to beg for mercy. Just then the King returned and shouted, "What? You will attack the Queen right in front of me?"

A eunuch quickly covered Haman's face. That meant Haman was already as good as dead. Another eunuch helpfully told the king that Haman had erected a tall pole in his garden to stick Mordecai on. "Good," said the King. "Stick Haman's body on that pole." It was done. Then Ahasuerus gave all of Haman's property to Mordecai, and made him the new Prime Minister.

But what was to be done about the King's edict to kill the Jews? The Persians had a rule that no law could ever be taken back. So King Asahuerus told Esther and Mordecai to write whatever they wanted, and he would sign it. They wrote, "All the Jews have the King's permission to gather and defend themselves against any attackers." The King's riders went swiftly to all 127 provinces of the Empire and posted this new message. The attackers would not be the King's army! When the day came, the Jews lived instead of dying, and they even killed some of their attackers.

Afterwards, Prime Minister Mordecai sent a letter to all the Jews in the Empire calling them to remember God's deliverance in a new feast named Purim. Jews celebrate it to this day in late winter. Jesus himself celebrated Purim (see John 5), the feast that remembers how God saved Israel through beautiful Queen Esther. Not just beautiful. She was also clever and brave. God had put her in the palace, just as he had once put Joseph in Egypt, to save his people when the time came. When that time came in Persia, Esther was ready to die if she had to. "If I perish, I perish," she said. But she lived, and by her courage God saved his People Israel from destruction.

Printed in the USA
CPSIA information can be obtained
at www.ICGtesting.com
CBHW071532040624
9558CB00005B/103